FOOTNOTES OF MERCY

poems by

Stephanie Brown

Finishing Line Press
Georgetown, Kentucky

FOOTNOTES OF MERCY

Copyright © 2018 by Stephanie Brown
ISBN 978-1-63534-444-8 First Edition
All rights reserved under International and Pan-American Copyright Conventions. No part of this book may be reproduced in any manner whatsoever without written permission from the publisher, except in the case of brief quotations embodied in critical articles and reviews.

ACKNOWLEDGMENTS

The poems listed below first appeared in the following publications.

Third Wednesday: The Dead Girls Admonish the Poet
Grey Sparrow Press: Doorstep of a Thousand Deaths
The Talking Stick; The Days the Trees Came Down (current title: After the Trees Came Down); Unbridaled; Bone
Evening Street Review: Blood Moon; City and Son, Far From Home; Everyday Heroes; There Will Be No Headline about You and Me
In the Company of Others: A Foreward Anthology: Moons across the Road

Publisher: Leah Maines
Editor: Christen Kincaid
Cover Art: Stephanie Brown
Author Photo: Monica Miller
Cover Design: Ryan W. Bradley

Printed in the USA on acid-free paper.
Order online: www.finishinglinepress.com
also available on amazon.com

Author inquiries and mail orders:
Finishing Line Press
P. O. Box 1626
Georgetown, Kentucky 40324
U. S. A.

Table of Contents

Invitation 1

In My Dreams 2

In Seconds 4

The Dead Girls Admonish the Poet 5

Empty Locket 6

City and Son, Far From Home 7

Girl with Cat 8

Blood Moon 10

Bone 12

The Caller 13

Everyday Heroes 17

Things We Say For Others 19

There Will Be No Headline about You and Me 20

Terribly Understood 21

The Poet Considers Possibility 22

Supporting Role 23

Moons across the Road 24

After the Trees Came Down 26

Doorstep of a Thousand Deaths 28

Unbridled 29

Rhapsody 30

For Tom, Hannah, and Austin

Invitation

Let's talk
   about the muse and me. How we show up
   unannounced. Our alliance isn't formal
but organic, with tension
   and flow. It helps to have music: thunderous
   tremolo from the Mississippi River, black lab

brio mixing with a Burmese chorus,
   and a fastoso duet by cardinal and crow,
effecting chaos, like a drunk
uncle whose havoc induces
   delight and private pain. So far,

no circus lions, ladies
   on horseback, or snakes. No physics
   or math invited to harness
disorder. Nothing about
   a Japanese tea garden with statue of Kannon,
   Goddess of Mercy. And then

   death
     with its audacity
appears without notice.

Dreams, art, and cities
   are welcome. I receive the energy of sin and summer,
   moles underground, in Levis and politics, hydrangeas
and hats. I delight in the unexpected
   entrances of garden gnomes, tumbleweed, fossils,
   heroes.

My tools readied,
   sharpened to excavate the fertile loam,
        rich and dark.

In My Dreams

      I walk down train tracks

         even when every muscle

yearns to run

   even when a deafening whistle warns me

            electrifies my flight response

   and rain, its spectral breath,

        blurs an already dim vista—

your outline fading,
fading.

      I stumble, try to stand,

  then fall on my face.

        My legs feel anchored in wet concrete.

          Your cries perforate the air.

    Like a wind-up toy

      I march to your rescue.

         One foot on the ground,

    the other mid-step

         but there's no one to rewind me.

Late again, late

   as your pleas

     dissipate.

In Seconds
> *for Jordan*

The vehicle of youth
crashes
like the Chevy Malibu.

Four college students undaunted
by the winter storm outside, safe
inside that womb of metal and rubber.

Those last moments—
time becomes chilled honey, smart
phones and iPods
swirl weightlessly, before flying
through broken glass.

Across the icy highway
her tattered canvas backpack
holds a Bible, her writing in the margins,
the ink of her uncrossed J
smeared.

The Dead Girls Admonish the Poet

Don't write about the snow
as an angel, as if
it is pure and gentle.

Don't write about the angel
as a guardian, as if
it intercedes with death.

Don't write about the wind
as a spirit, as if
it imparts deliverance.

No. Write instead
about when we were fugitive youth.
Write about the rim, the edge, the end;
about lesions of despair.

Write about what is lost, what is found
in the landfills of grief.
No footnote of comfort. No footnote of mercy.

Write about the blue hour
when the lunacy of truth enters
into the dreams of the living.

Blue Hour: The period of twilight each morning and evening. Also called *sweet light*. The French spoke of the blue hour as a time of confusion and mystery.

Empty Locket

November wind
shuffles each leaf
like playing cards in spokes
pedaled rapidly.
Bikes can save you
when you are small and without
power.

A rusty locket
discarded at marsh's edge,
reveals emptiness.

Tiny nest in the crotch between two thin branches.

Our nest is empty—
we are supposed to be sad,
instead we have time.

Dried oak leaves,
birch twigs, dog crap
on the tar path—remnants—
sometimes
that's all there is to work with.

Endless fascination
with the generous sky of blue
with distances
content with the whole, yet

distressed
by the pieces
leftovers
and what has been lost.

City and Son, Far From Home

Suitcases arrive, heaped with ambition.

The iconic Hollywood sign represents possibility; draws
creative people here. Homes are embedded

in the hills. Helicopter din replaces
the ambulance sirens you heard in Chicago.

Sidewalks are empty, except where stars fall and costumed
characters pimp themselves; where sometimes, tourists fall too.

We walk your dog to the farmers market on Sunset in search
of blood oranges and mangos, make our way past flyers,

flattened Tecate cans, and condom wrappers
tossed near chipped curbs. Cars squat,

abandoned on narrow streets. We drive out
of the city to Santa Monica Beach where waves

lick shorelines and sunburned toes, spit out Frisbees.
Soon we are cruising for record shops and I grow

wistful for the early years when you had an umbilical
attachment to music. Standing together in Amoeba

Records, we flip through sleeves of memory—Quietdrive,
Motion City Soundtrack, Atmosphere. Each day

a new place to walk where odors assault us—mint and sage,
sweet weed smoke, citrus, enchiladas, salt and piss.

Try to love it, you say, just like you love me.

Girl with Cat
    Balthus, 1934

There is a slate-colored cat with stripes.
But this is about the girl.

Ten years old, maybe thirteen, reclining
against an emerald cushion on a wooden chaise,
hands clasped behind her head of ringed curls.
A headband matches her skirt of tiffany blue.
Her shirt, a faded pink, stretches flat across her chest. Legs
bare down to the brown-checked socks slipped into
gray Mary Janes. One foot is on the floor,
the other is bent and poised on the chaise. Her skirt spreads
back to her hips, revealing white panties.
Balthus has given her contoured eyebrows, full lips, a seductive
slant in the corner of her eyes. Remember when

> there were dirt fields for pick-up games or a slick
> of ice to skate on all day? The weather didn't matter
> because there was exploring to do: salamander hunts,
> clover picking, fort building, bike races. Nights
> of Kick the Can and stolen kisses during Hide and Seek
> until porch lights blinked like fireflies, signaling an end
> to the day. Remember when all in one day,
> you could play Candyland and smoke cigarettes
> with your best friend as you contemplate
> having sex with your boyfriend? There is a skinny teenage girl

staring at the painting hung on a solitary wall. Skin tight
black jeans, pilling gray sweater, shabby ballet shoes,
no socks. Her arms wrap around her waist, nail-bitten fingers sprout
like tiny wings from her ribs. She is crying.

She roams the dimly lit hallways alone, stopping
for a long time near the Thorne Miniature rooms. I think how
at fourteen I had to move and my cat ran away,
leaving warm indentations all over the old house
like little graves.

Blood Moon
> *In 1924, Carrie Buck was selected…to test the legality…*
> *of Virginia's Eugenical Sterilization Act*
> Claude Moore Health Science Library

In a sterile room with manufactured light,
white floor tiles, and counter tops cold as disinfected
tools on the tray. Disguised by clean butcher

paper, the bed creaks as the quaking young girl
lies down. Her chest heaves, inhaling
an antiseptic fate. Raped

at seventeen and blamed for it. Foster
parents committed her after the birth
of her baby; a facade to shift blame. It's the men

who ran the colony for people they deemed degenerate
and shiftless, who defended their actions
as duty to serve the whole. It's the men

who judged her, cut her, challenged her right
to live as a valued person; who considered Carrie
and her mother Emma, menaces to society. It's the men

who used science to justify their abuse,
passed laws to stop the spread of imbeciles.
Forgive the men who committed your mother,

your daughter, you—three generations condemned.
Forgive the women, the teachers and nurses who obeyed
the men. Three years of feeble attempts to save her fertility.

Carrie has lost. Doctors wear pristine scrubs, hiding
dark madness underneath. No mother or nurse to hold
her hand. No one to explain her barren future.

Her eyes close. Her back, soft and damp.
She wilts, an exploited rose.

Forgive the moon its sanguine nature.
Forgive me for stopping here.

Bone

The couple drives along, leisure in their pockets,
two months before summer's swell of crowds.

They've become part of the plein-air scene
Riccoboni paints—*Beach on Coronado Island.*

The Silver Strand current ferries in mica. Thousands
of tiny, glittering gold mirrors, cast onto her lover's

bare feet, reflecting the face of a younger
self, animated with curiosity. He calls to her

and points to a white object half in the dune.
She gently tugs and discovers a bone.

She rotates it around, rubs her thumb over
flecks of mica clinging to its sponge-like ends,

finds the perfect heart in the bone's center.
Look at this! she exclaims. A passing glance

is all he affords: *Why would you save something
like* that? His disgust triggers an undertow of shame.

She watches him seize the artist's brush, dip it in matte
black, paint over her pastel paradise. The slate

blue sky disappears, then the gulls. He ridicules her
delight and there go the rocks, the shoreline, the glitter.

His mocking continues and she feels herself
shrink as she walks toward the bruised reef,

the bone, a pale shadow, her back painted black.

The Caller
> *Unlean against our hearts*
> Kay Ryan "Blandeur"

Today I remember
  the caller, her anguish
    palpable
  across phone lines
as she begs for help to find
              a home.

> *I have to move from hotel*
> *to hotel, my stuff*
> *scattered*
> *in small towns across Minnesota*
> *and I haven't slept*
> *for days. Who can sleep in a hotel?*

She's forgotten
those nights as a child
rising to her name, Ellen, Ellen …
singing to calm her mother; a lily
in a vase without water.

> *I'm sick of people*
> *who pawn me*
> *   from one organization*
> *to the next. I'm like*
> *   the goddamn ball*
> *in a pinball machine.*

She wanted sisters
    but has none.
        And the men in her life,
    well, she can't stay with the men.
          They get her in trouble.
    She's an orphan of circumstance.

Dash is my only
    companion, but he barks
too much and gets us kicked out
    of hotels.

One year from today
there will be an unbearable
silence, but in this moment
she muzzles the dog

I've called
    all the resources on my list
    more than once.
I just know
    they keep count of my calls.

She keens on
    about aid agencies
  who conspire against her.

> *God*
> *they won't give me an inch!*
> *What do they expect me to do?*

Whole notes of ruin repeat
then sustain in her life, the musical
rescue she could once create
is gone.

.

> *I really need food*
> *and Dash has to eat too.*
> *Maybe he wouldn't bark so much*
> *if he wasn't hungry.*

I give her directions
to our food shelf—

> *I don't*
> *have a car! If only*
> *I had a sister to drive me.*
> *Can't you take care of me, for once?*

For once, the words
she uses each time she calls.

Clients are lining up
  and taking their number.
    I move the phone
      to my other ear.
She moves swiftly
    to the subject of finding work.

> *I'll wait tables, wash dishes,*
> *sweep floors, even*
> *clean toilets,*
> *but I am not*
> *applying on a computer!*
> *That is not*
> *how you get a job!*

I have no reply. Silence,
    then she lifts the needle back
      to the beginning.
   I have to say goodbye. I hear her dog
       barking
     as she begins to sing
        Hush little baby, don't say a word…

Everyday Heroes

    I.
The cashiers
at Stevens Grocery
have their personal sorrows
but smile
at the man who blames them
for the price of groceries,
apologizing
each time he comes through the line.

Cashiers face customers
unhinged
because their favorite oatmeal
or brand of coffee
has been moved or discontinued.
They want something constant in their lives.
The cashiers know this and serve
as a steadfast presence.

    II.
The librarians
reiterate the fine for an overdue book
to an unrepentant woman.
She regards
their appeal for payment with suspicion.
The librarians are polite as they display
the evidence before them.

Lonely patrons
find escape in a gripping novel
and linger
desperate for connection.

The librarians
accept their need,
extend daily compassion.

    III.
The waitresses
absorb the blame
for undercooked meals, weak drinks,
all the unfairness in our world.
With the strength of Atlas,
they shoulder the weight
of each person's
irritation.

Clattering dishes compete
with the chatter of customers
seated at their usual table
day after day
confiding their secrets,
with a hunger for absolution.
The waitresses respond with endless
cups of coffee.

The Things We Say For Others

Every day the nurse says the same thing: *I think
he's going to go on this shift.* Four days of fever,
no food, lungs filling up; each breath
like percolating coffee.

Oxygen and hourly hits of morphine—my friend
has been dying for days.

The minister keeps telling me: *I don't think
it'll be long* and Karen from hospice palliates,
I think he's happy. I think he's happy.
We're all guilty of making predictions, offering empty promises:

>   *You'll feel better with time.
>   After some sleep, you'll be fine.*

I sit holding his warm hand, massage
certainty from his slack arms, swap
washcloths of assurance from his forehead
and chest, with ones of cool comfort.

Grateful for the noon hour
when residents and staff are at lunch,
leaving us time to release the braided reins
of past and present;
echoes and gold.

There Will Be No Headline about You and Me

From a table lit
by three burning wicks
of a blueberry candle, I gaze
at our old birch tree and its emerging
buds of pale green.
From the radio
another grim report
about texting, how emoticons are replacing
real emotion—a genuine smile,
wink, or grimace—
allowing us to forget how
looking into another face
is not a burden.

> *Wait.*
> *Wait.*

I want to take your hand
and sit near the old birch tree,
explore your thoughts
in the solitude of our own backyard.

I want to hear your satisfied sigh
while we watch the sun vanish,
turning the blueberry sky to black.

We'll be unrestrained
under the stars—like shimmering bonfires.

Hide our secrets
in the hollows of the birch
until they burn to bits of ash.

Terribly Understood

It's unsettling being known
more than I want to admit.
You see through
the protective devices I thought
hidden—my inclination
to dodge
with practiced humility,
with seasoned evasion; the way
I am adept at listening in order
to avoid being heard.

The Poet Considers Possibility

As a young child I learned to speak
using only the necessary words;
the abridged account.

Patience was limited
and time even more so. Lack of
interest in substance or imagination
propelled me to the final lines; the moral
of the story.

Now I am learning
to fill in the space between words
with more words; to make something
from what I believed was worth nothing.

I found others willing
to hear an entire narrative.

Yet when I write, it is with economy

though at times when more is requested,
I have faith in what's beyond
the short version.

Supporting Role

Crow is dressed for concealment
like a teenager at a Marilyn Manson concert.
Harbors a fondness for what is shiny.

Cardinal is always cast
as the lead. His star qualities:
flashy carmine cape,
sable mask of mystery
extending to chin and throat,
the constant pronouncement

I am here-here-here
delivered with a chippy exuberance
that softens the harshest critic.

Crow rallies the crowd
as the warm-up act
with comic impressions—blue jay
screams, song sparrow refrains,
phoebe's self-important
repetition of her name.

Crow knows
how its purple sheen
glimmers in sunlight
for anyone willing to look beyond
its ebony disguise.

Moons across the Road

Her shell a ridged
disc
thirteen olive grey
moons
each its own season
called to life
by naming:
harvest moon
snow moon
sturgeon moon
blue…
Snapping turtle mother
heavy with eggs,
and moon cycles
to count.

She is rugged,
enchanting;
her retractable
head, thick
with accordion wrinkles,
her pointed snout
and toothless grin,
deceptively safe,
her ragged warrior gloves,
curved claws.

Her bony carriage
must cross
a paved frontier
designed
for the swift
who have no regard
for the sacred.

Here
moons have been
crushed.
Will others
racing through this street
swerve, slow down,
or stop to watch her
as I did?

I say: Let clouds
envelope her
in a dream world
where wind's cool
palm carries her
close to the sun
for basking.

I say: Let her
open mouth
exhale
a footpath of stars
guiding her safely
to the other side.

In some Native American cultures it is believed that the thirteen scales on a turtle's shell stand for the thirteen cycles of the moon, each with its own name and story.

After the Trees Came Down

            First
I see trimmed boardwalk maples
and remind myself—*This was your decision.*
It's hard to look at those gaunt bodies,
their gold caps that used to shade street
edges where dog shit and deer scat
are found.

            Next
I turn to our house on the hill,
grip tight on the wheel as my car
crawls up the spare sleeve of driveway.
No shadows now from stray sumac,
or the tangled branches of birch
and red oak.

            Then
sawdust graves become visible.
Shade garden is missing its muse,
its skeleton companion destroyed
so that flavescent hostas sink
into the gap. *What have I done?*

            And
farther up, part of the squirrels'
playground and roof access is lost.
Four cavities remain where the white
oak canopy once cooled our black lab
for thirteen summers.

        Now
another absence where we used to place
the kiddie pool, under the shade
of the black walnut tree.
The tree had grown taller, lankier,
and leaned away from home,
as teenagers do.

        Later
my knees will buckle and I will fall
to the ground, claw at the ruined earth
and plead for winter to come, to weep
its white gauze over these fresh sores.

Doorstep of a Thousand Deaths

Sweeping grit and shags of oak leaves from the concrete
steps unveils splotches of small rust-colored stains;
evidence of a June bug massacre.
Slivers of red-brown shells and shreds of wing
spied among patio rocks. Luna moth clings to the house
as if drunk on porch light. One June bug survivor
on its back, three pairs of legs kicking like a helpless baby.
Spare him from being gutted by the downy woodpecker.
Bend down and with a tender nudge, help it to its feet. Watch
as it toddles across the cold cement on exhausted legs.
Be happy
for the one life you can save.

Unbridaled

She is a sun goddess filly
shaking lemon glitter
grains from wild elflocks,
muzzle waggling like a bobble head.
She dances near bristle-backed
hay bales and rusted tractors.
Her legs
crease at the hock
then kick toward heaven.
Whinnies of liberty
escape on the breeze.

As I drive closer, my presence stifles
her fancy-free groove, slows her
to a common trot.
Just a horse now,
waiting to frolic. Idling
at the bend in the road,
I wait for her to show me that abandon.
I need her to show me.

Driving away, I look
in my rearview mirror and see her
dance again.
Coral tinted sundogs
remind me how distance
can allow others to shine.

Rhapsody

Praise glad voices
   resonating
for all to hear.
Praise the kind word,
   a lavish token
placed gently in your palm.

Praise each life
graced with longevity
   or abundant
despite its brevity.

Praise your partner's
steady hand extended
   with merciful devotion,
despite your inadequacies.

Praise the friends
who replenish you
   fondly
through all the dark nonfictions
forming your story.

Praise murmured
invocations, longings,
and the quiet
moon-brilliance that is your life.

About the cover art

Cairns are a tradition from ancient cultures often erected for navigation, spiritual offering, as an act of service, or as monuments of remembrance. Poems are created for these reasons as well. Cairns and poems take many forms and whether you are new to poetry or have a long relationship with it, may one word, image or phrase, like one stone, leave its mark.

ADDITIONAL ACKNOWLEDGEMENTS

My appreciation for the Loft Literary Center of Minneapolis and all the outstanding poetry instructors I've been fortunate to study with. Special thanks to Carol Bjorlie, Roseanne Lloyd and Deborah Keenan for their guidance when I was a beginner. My deepest gratitude to Thomas R. Smith who helped shape me as a poet by being gracious, inspiring, and for knowing when to push. His insights and knowledge guided the work in this manuscript. My *Forward* peers were keen advisors along the way. Thanks to: Jim Bettendorf, Sue Crouse, Barb Draper, Sandy Larson, Kristi Laurel, Leslie Matton-Flynn, Ardie Medina, LeRoy Sorenson, Bill Upjohn, and Miriam Weinstein. Sincere appreciation to Jude Nutter for her skillful instruction and wisdom. Most importantly, my love and thanks to Tom for his enduring support and his unwavering belief in me.

Stephanie attended Minnesota State University—Mankato and earned a Bachelor of Arts degree in Elementary Education with a minor in Special Education. She taught first grade for a number of years in public and private schools before deciding to stay home to raise her children.

Stephanie began journaling as a young parent which ultimately led her to taking writing classes at The Loft Literary Center of Minneapolis. She dabbled in fiction and children's literature before finding her place in poetry. In 2011 she was accepted into *The Forward Program*, a two-year program that included individual mentoring and peer group interaction and study. She continues to meet with the 10 members of this peer group who collaborated on an anthology released in 2017 titled *In the Company of Others*.

Stephanie has lived in Minnesota all her life and has great affection for the delights and nuisances of every season this state offers. She and her husband Tom reside in Elk River where Stephanie volunteers, tends her garden and writes anywhere there is a window for gazing.

www.ingramcontent.com/pod-product-compliance
Lightning Source LLC
LaVergne TN
LVHW041554070426
835507LV00011B/1076